Virginia Page
10 Glamorgan Road
Hatherley
Cheltenham GL51 3JF
Tel. 01242 701886

# Designs from HISTORIC TEXTILES

*Jan Messent*

Front cover : detail of 'The Otter and Swan Hunt' from the Devonshire Tapestries. 15th century. Flemish.
Back cover: part of the Elizabeth Haines embroidery seen on p.35 with two figures from the same period.

Loosely-woven linen mesh border of vine leaves and grapes. Italian 17th century.

## Ancient Egypt

Tapestry-woven pattern from Tutankhamun's glove.
1334 – 1325 B.C.

Motifs from tapestry-woven fabric : Tuthmosis IV
1419 – 1386 B.C.

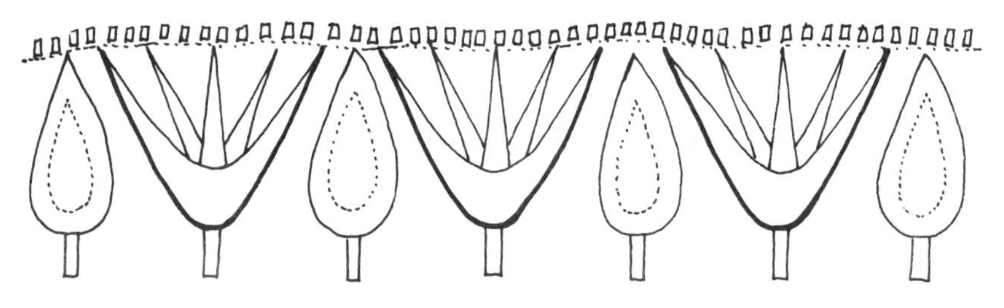

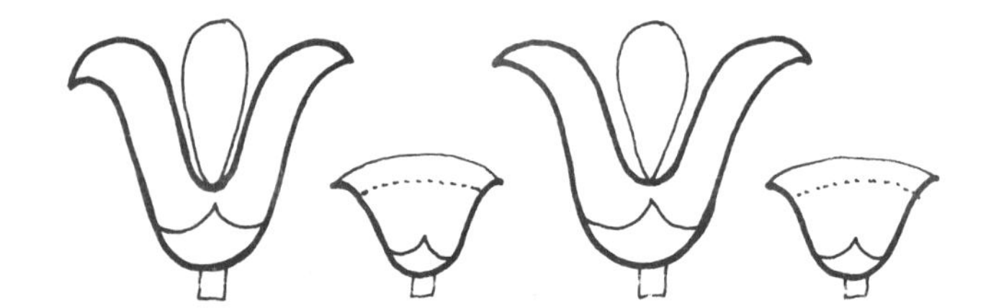

No weavers in the ancient world surpassed the Egyptians. Tapestry-weaving was practiced at an early date : the earliest surviving pieces belong to the period 1541 – 1481 B.C. and are woven entirely of linen. The design is alike on both sides of the fabric.

"I have decked my bed with coverings of tapestry with carved works, and fine linen of Egypt."

Exodus ch.36 v.37

Egyptian tapestry pattern from a tomb at Thebes : musicians and dancers.

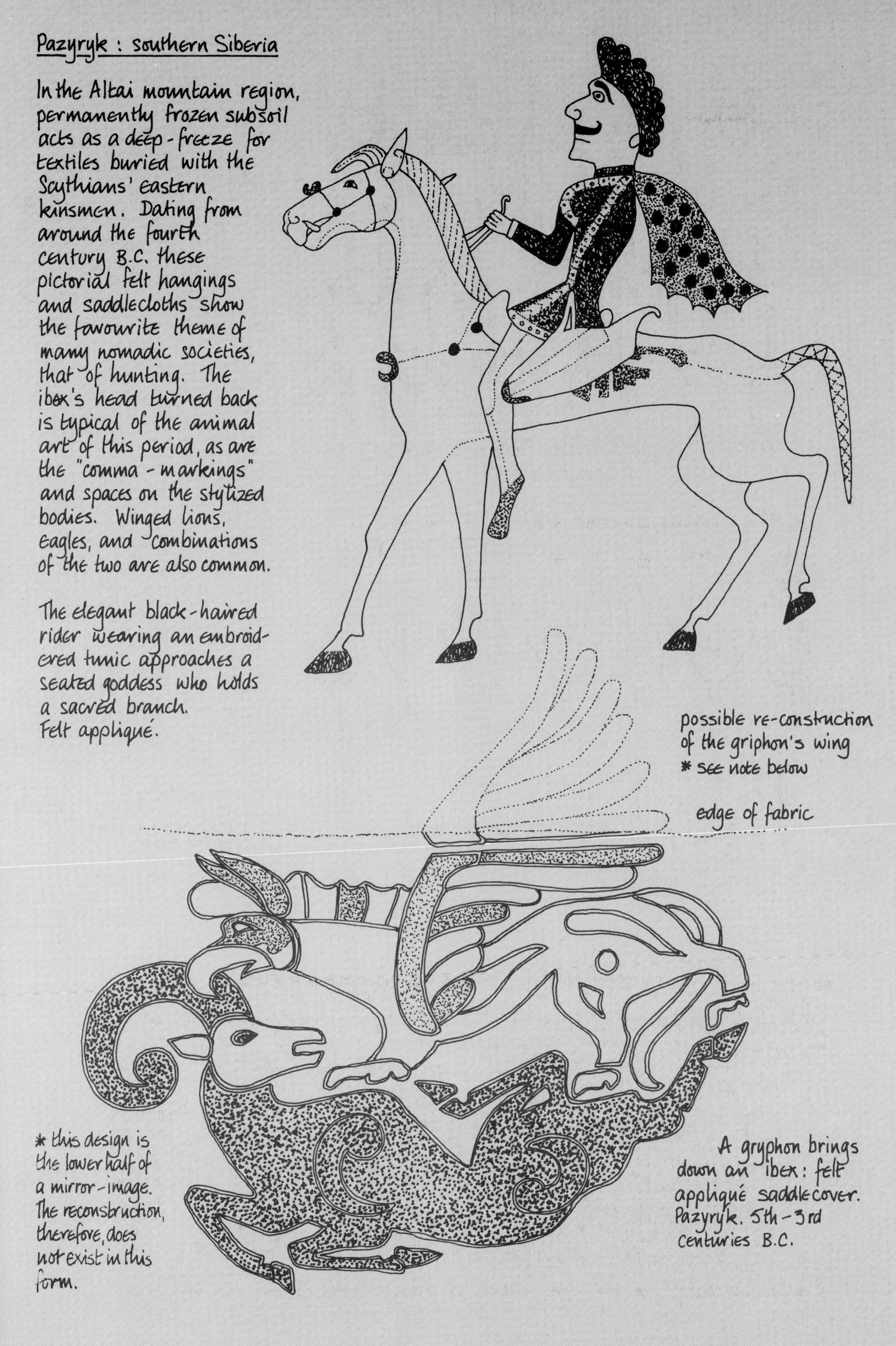

## Pazyryk : southern Siberia

In the Altai mountain region, permanently frozen subsoil acts as a deep-freeze for textiles buried with the Scythians' eastern kinsmen. Dating from around the fourth century B.C. these pictorial felt hangings and saddlecloths show the favourite theme of many nomadic societies, that of hunting. The ibex's head turned back is typical of the animal art of this period, as are the "comma-markings" and spaces on the stylized bodies. Winged lions, eagles, and combinations of the two are also common.

The elegant black-haired rider wearing an embroidered tunic approaches a seated goddess who holds a sacred branch.
Felt appliqué.



A gryphon brings down an ibex: felt appliqué saddle cover. Pazyryk. 5th - 3rd centuries B.C.

* this design is the lower half of a mirror-image. The reconstruction, therefore, does not exist in this form.

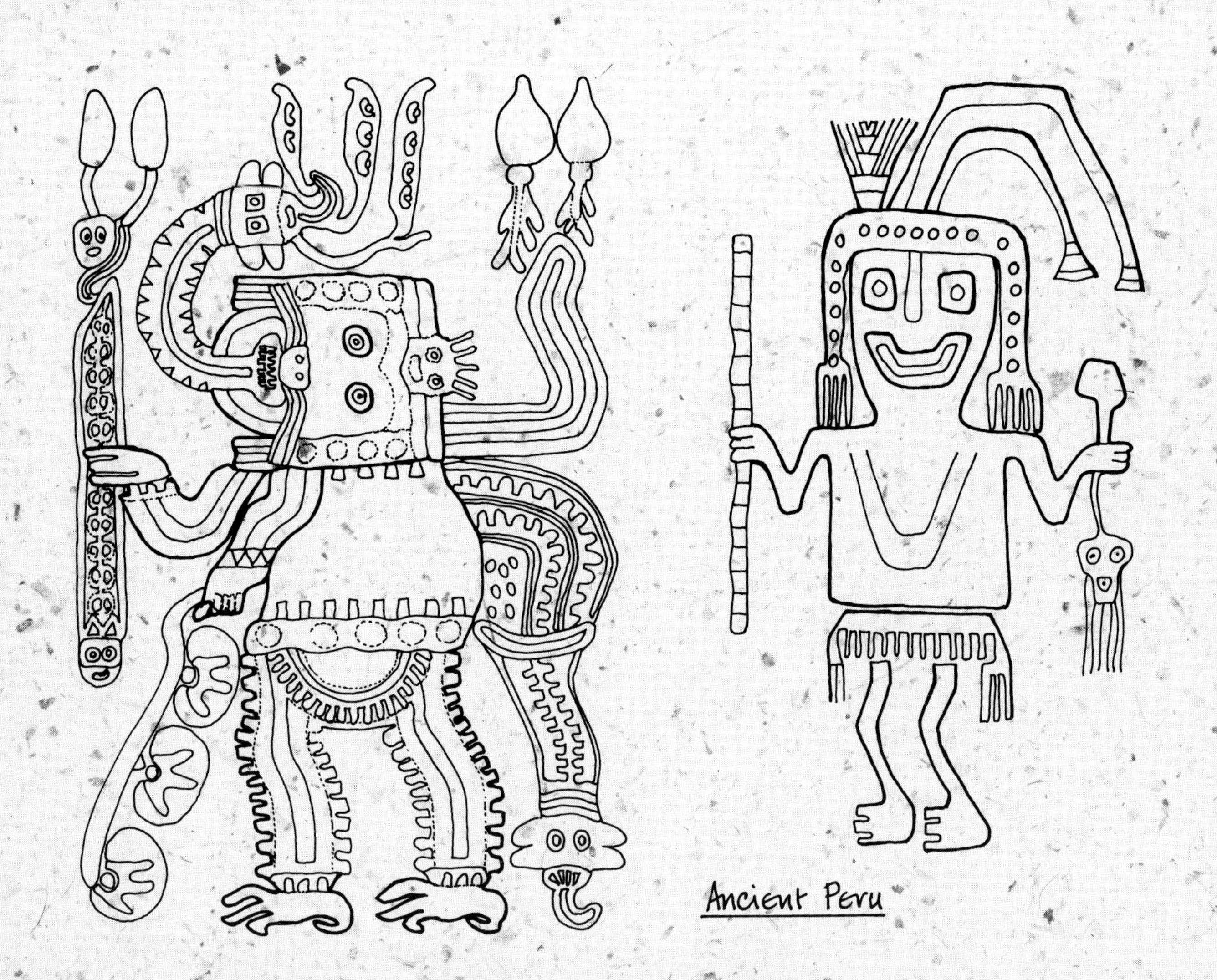


Mantles, woven and embroidered by the natives of the Paracas Peninsula, are unique in the history of textiles. The dead were wrapped in these mantles, the dry desert sand creating ideal conditions for their preservation. Measuring 8 ft. x $4\frac{1}{2}$ ft. they were made specifically for burial and are covered by rows (or chequered) of densely-embroidered fantastic figures, some in a naturalistic style, as shown by the two figures above, and some in a more geometric style, as seen by the two birds below.

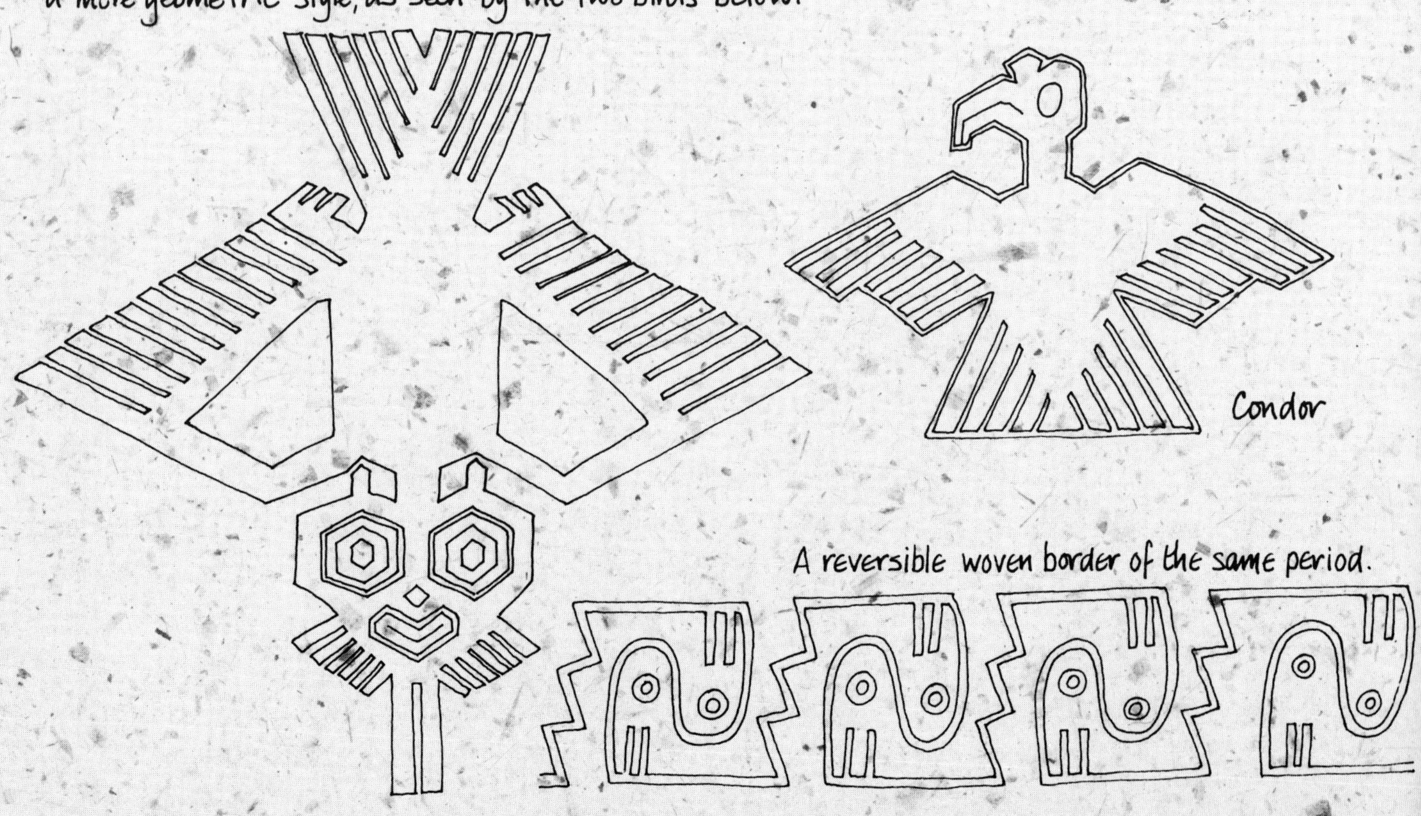

The textile arts of Peru were well-established long before the arts of pottery-making or goldsmithing: the oldest textile patterns yet discovered originate from around 2000 B.C. Though worked on simple looms, the weaving techniques are both varied and complex. Pieces were either constructed to the size required, not cut, or several pieces of different techniques sewn together.

Each culture had its own distinctive style. The design shown here dates from between 500 and 900 A.D. and is taken from a cotton and wool Tiahuanaco tapestry measuring 9 ins (23 cms) high. It shows the snarling head of a jaguar with two more highly-stylized bodies at each side.

(Museum fur Volkerkunde. Munich.)

Coptic Textiles
A simplified drawing of a roundel, tapestry-woven into the front of a linen and wool Coptic tunic between the 4th and 5th centuries. The Copts were native Egyptian Christians. Their tunics were ornamented by tapestry-woven borders and roundels. Some of these would be made by →
needleweaving on the warp threads left empty for the purpose.
Three of the most decorative elements have been isolated and used to make borders. Many other variations are possible.

Above: a typically formal design of birds facing each other across a Tree of Life. Griffins, lions and dragons are other favourites.
As Persian weavers were highly-skilled, many of them were employed in countries where they were influenced by the designs of foreign craftsmen.
This Persian silk dates from the 8th–9th century.

Top left: a cockerel motif from a Persian silk of 8th–10th century.

Left: a tapestry of gold and silk of figures with a Tree of Life. Islamic-Sicilian work c. 1100 A.D.

A reconstructed detail from a fragmented tapestry frieze found in the Oseberg burial chamber, Norway, in 1903. With the body of an aristocratic young lady were weaving tools and a tapestry which shows a procession of armed figures, male and female, accompanied by horse-drawn wagons. It was woven in coloured wools and is dated to the year 834 A.D. by the tree-ring dating of the oaks used to construct the burial chamber.

Norway c. 1180 A.D.

A gaily-coloured fragment of tapestry showing the month of April, made to cover pews in the church at **Baldishol**, Norway. It now belongs to the Museum of Antiquities, Oslo, Norway. The background colour of this vividly patterned piece is a bold red with broken geometric shapes of beige, probably faded from yellow. The figure wears a patterned blue/white divided gown, and the word (A)PRIILIS can be seen on the archway above his head.

## English goldwork. 10th Century

Durham Cathedral. England.

John the Baptist holds a palm and a book.

From the maniple of Saint Cuthbert, the figures of Peter the Deacon and John the Baptist.
32·25 ins × 2·4 ins.
The maniple depicts popes and attendant deacons on either side of a central quatrefoil. The half-figure above appears on one of the end panels with John the Evangelist at the other end.

Worked in coloured silks and silver-gilt thread in stem and split stitches and couching, the Durham vestments are the earliest pieces of embroidery to survive in England and the only extant Anglo-Saxon embroideries, apart from the Bayeux Tapestry, to show human figures. They were made at the command of Queen Aelfflaed, who died in 916, for Frithestan, Bishop of Winchester from 909 to 931.

## Anglo-Saxon Embroidery

## Motifs from the Bayeux Tapestry

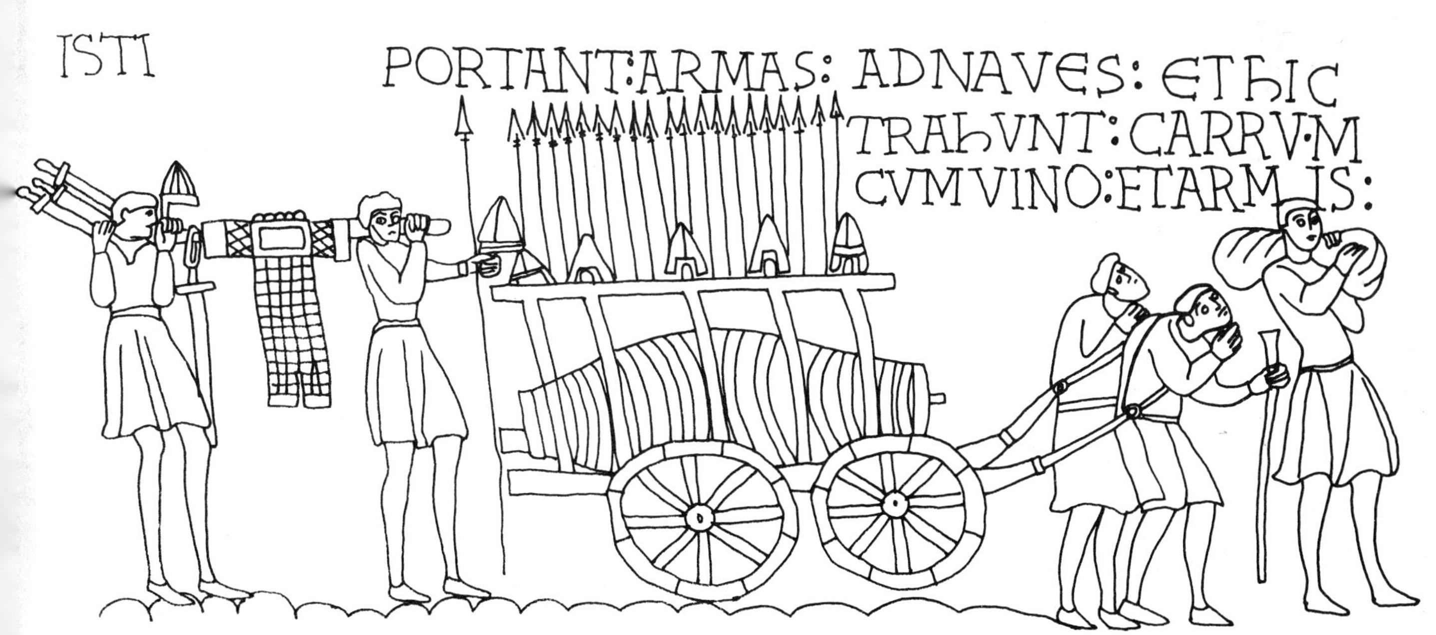


Though always referred to as a tapestry, this is an embroidery of wool on linen measuring 230ft. 9 ins x 18–20 ins. Worked by English embroiderers for Bishop Odo of Bayeux shortly after the Battle of Hastings in 1066 A.D., it commemorates the victory of Duke William of Normandy over King Harold of England.

Bishop Odo and Count Robert of Mortain are seen at the top left in council with their half-brother William. In the lower scene, men prepare for battle with suits of mail, weapons, food and drink.

Above: two compartments from the Malterer Hanging of c. 1310–20 given by the Malterer family to the convent where their daughter was a nun. The scenes show the dangers of earthly love, one (presumably) of being dropped from a great height, the second of being interrupted while at work with a torch of fire in one's hand. Dangers indeed! *

VBI: VNVS : CLERICVS : ET:
ÆLFGY VA

Right: the scene from the Bayeux Tapestry of Aelfgyva with the cleric shows a similar gesture of affection as the one above. The depiction of people in buildings with the walls removed was common from Anglo-Saxon times and throughout the middle ages.

* Phyllis and Aristotle

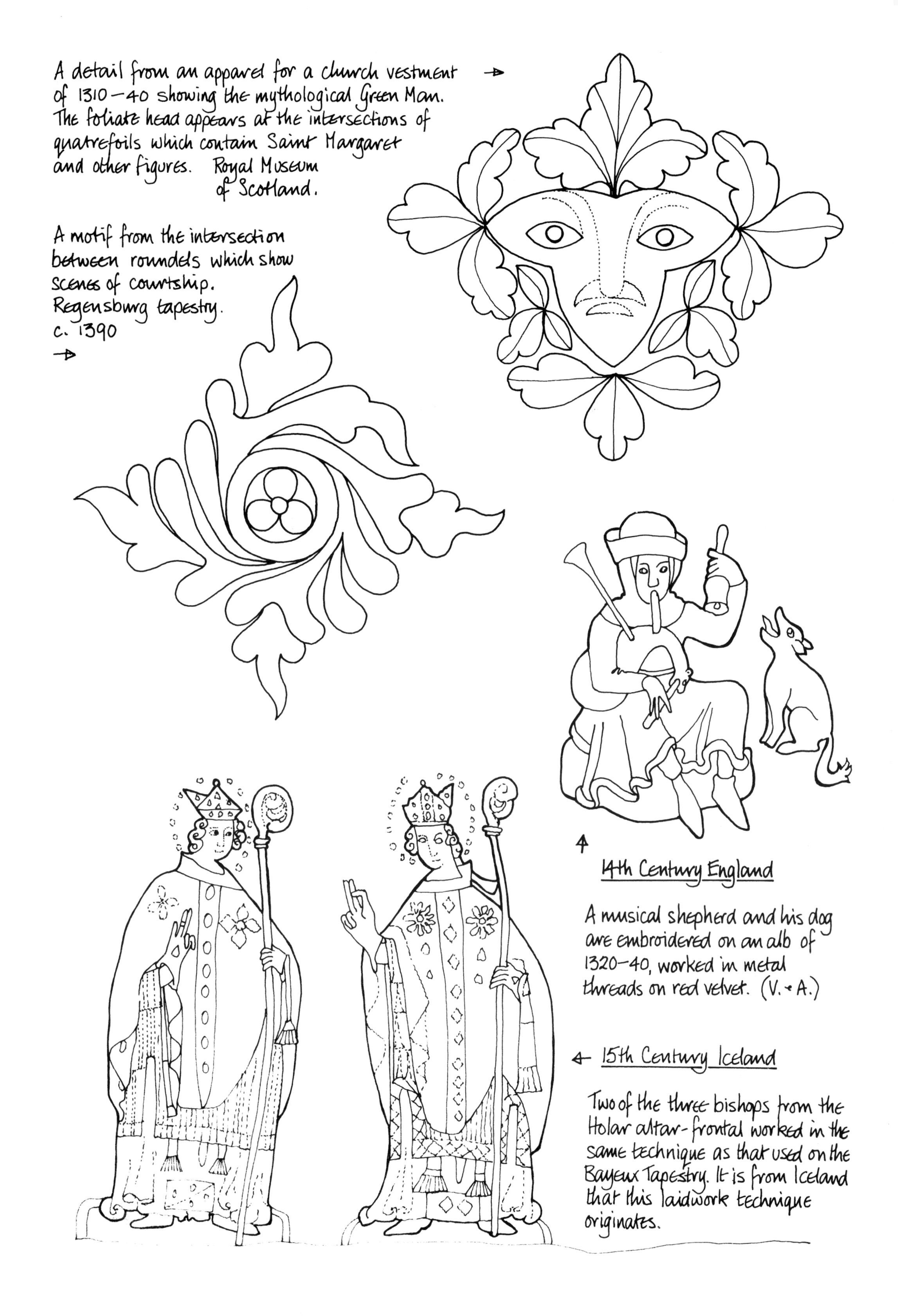

A detail from an apparel for a church vestment of 1310–40 showing the mythological Green Man. The foliate head appears at the intersections of quatrefoils which contain Saint Margaret and other figures. Royal Museum of Scotland.

A motif from the intersection between roundels which show scenes of courtship. Regensburg tapestry. c. 1390

14th Century England

A musical shepherd and his dog are embroidered on an alb of 1320–40, worked in metal threads on red velvet. (V. & A.)

15th Century Iceland

Two of the three bishops from the Holar altar-frontal worked in the same technique as that used on the Bayeux Tapestry. It is from Iceland that this laidwork technique originates.

Top left: detail of an embroidered chasuble orphrey showing King David tuning his harp. English: 1310 – 1340

Above: the orphrey of a cope (detail) showing an angel and Saint Catherine. English embroidery. 1340 – 70

Left: a simplified detail from the Steeple Ashton cope of the mid 13th – early 14th century, showing a symbol of the universe with creatures of earth, air and water.

The Guicciardini Quilt.

Squares and borders show scenes from the Tristan legend, the oppression of Cornwall by King Languis of Ireland and his champion the Morold. It is believed to be Sicilian work of c. 1400.

It is interesting to note how, perhaps due to a lack of understanding the design by the embroiderers, the knight's left hand has been lost in the pattern on his armour and his body has disappeared into the saddle-cloth. Also, the rower has been given two left arms, an error which could be the result of working the design upside-down or in poor light.

# The Devonshire Hunting Tapestries

A set of four fifteenth-century tapestries which came from the estate of the Dukes of Devonshire and which probably belonged at one time to the Countess of Shrewsbury, better known as Bess of Hardwick.

It is thought that they may have been made either at Arras or Tournai and would have been somewhat larger than their present dimensions of around 14 ft. high by (up to) 36 ft. wide.

Each tapestry shows a crowded hunt scene: here, the miller's wife is from 'Falconry', as is the proud rider on the back (inside) cover. The lady by his side appears in 'The Boar and Bear Hunt' and the bear on the front cover is from 'The Otter and Swan Hunt.' The other tapestry is 'The Deer Hunt,' and all four hang in the Victoria and Albert Museum, London.

The definitive book on the subject is now out of print. "The Devonshire Hunting Tapestries" is by George Wingfield Digby and Wendy Hefford. Published by the V & A. in 1971

ISBN 11 290037 2

## Medieval Tapestry Weaving

Dyers used huge vats over furnaces to colour large quantities of fabric, and wool tied in hanks. Only plant dyes were used at this time, some home-grown, some imported. It was a highly-specialised trade where strict rules were applied, one of which was that the use of woad, because of its appalling smell, could not be used inside the city walls.

Weavers of tapestry were more often men than women, but there were also itinerant weavers who went from one castle to another to weave 'in situ.' No doubt guests would see the work in progress and order

hangings for their halls there and then.

The tapissiere would sit square-on, not as shown here, and work from the back, each small section being built up block by block rather than from side to side in one throw. Each coloured yarn is wound onto a small pointed bobbin which hangs from the side nearest the worker, ready to be picked up when needed. Larger pieces would be made with the design running sideways and with more than one weaver.

Tapestries showing hunting scenes, biblical stories, mythology, the seasons, day to day life and favourite legends would hang from hooks or rings to warm and to brighten the cold stone walls, to divide rooms and to create privacy around beds. At each move from one castle to another, the tapestries would be taken down, rolled up, and carried on carts with the rest of the furniture.

Three foxes
Rabbits
Goat
Sheep
Unidentified, but may be big cats used for hunting.

## The Lady and the Unicorn

A set of six tapestries sold to the Cluny Museum in 1882. On a red background, and thickly scattered with flowers, the Lady, the Lion and the Unicorn appear in each one depicting Sight, Sound, Tasre, Touch and Smell, the sixth depicting the idea of a gift. They were made in the 15th C. and given as a gift to a young bride by her betrothed. Her arms are on each of the panels. Animals appear everywhere, all at peace with each other.

Except for the unicon and initials, all the motifs on these two pages belong to this set.

## The Unicorn Tapestries

Although made in the same century, this set of seven tapestries belongs to the Cloisters of the Metropolitan Museum of Art, New York. It depicts allegorical scenes of a unicorn hunt. Like the Cluny tapestries, this set was also made for a bride by her new husband, but they are quite different in style, being full of vigour and activity, except for the last.

1. The Hunt Begins.
2. The Unicorn at the Fountain.
3. The Unicorn Leaps into the Stream.
4. The Unicorn Defends Himself
5. (only two fragments) The Unicorn is Captured by the Maiden.
6. He is Killed and Brought to the Castle.
7. The Unicorn in Captivity. Inside a fened enclosure, he is brought to life and tamed, chained to a tree. The entwined initials AE appear in all seven tapestries.

In the middle ages, representations of the mythical unicorn were not uncommon. There were frequent references to them in bestiaries, described in one as Honorius Augustodunensis, horse's body, stag's head, goat's beard, cloven hooves, lion's tail and a single horn (twisted) 4ft. long which was invested with the power to detect poison.

Sixteenth Century

Three fruit tree motifs set within frames of twisting foliage with wild beasts at their bases. The designs were drawn onto canvas in ink ready for tent stitch.

Opposite page: a chart based on a design of cushion-covers embroidered by Mary, Queen of Scots incorporating the national emblems of France, Scotland and England. In tent stitch, silk on linen, with gold and silver threads.

The design of the original version, now at Hardwick Hall in Derbyshire, is scattered with more naturalistic foliage and small applied roundels containing fables that comment upon her imprisoned state.

Thistles: the tops are striped in two tones of mauve. The bases are chequered two tones of green.
Lilies: creamy-white petals with pink ⊡. Green stems and leaves, yellow or gold stamens.
Roses: white petals, pink ⊠, yellow and white centres, yellow or gold ⧄.
Twisted cords: ⧄ indicates gold or silver on a yellow or grey cord.
Background: the original is yellow, but the choice is yours. Bear in mind that the flower-heads are relatively pale.

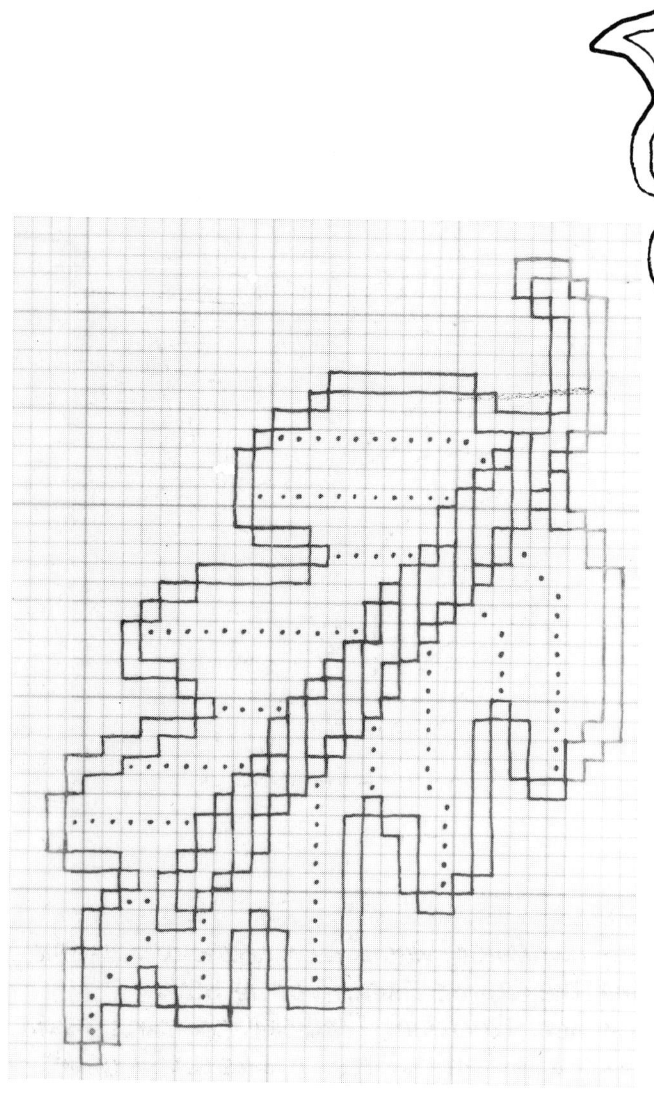

An oak leaf motif from a cushion-cover worked in tent stitch on a dark red background of long-armed cross stitch.

This simple motif may easily be translated onto squared paper as shown and used alone or in a pattern like the original below.

Hardwick Hall, Derbyshire.

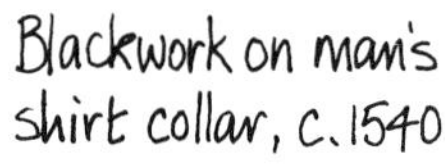
Blackwork on man's shirt collar, c.1540

Elizabeth, Countess of Shrewsbury, (1520–1608), better known as Bess of Hardwick, was a keen needlewoman who, while befriending the captive Mary, Queen of Scots, embroidered with her. Hardwick Hall still contains many embroidered pieces and tapestries, and this small plant motif is from a larger piece mounted in velvet.

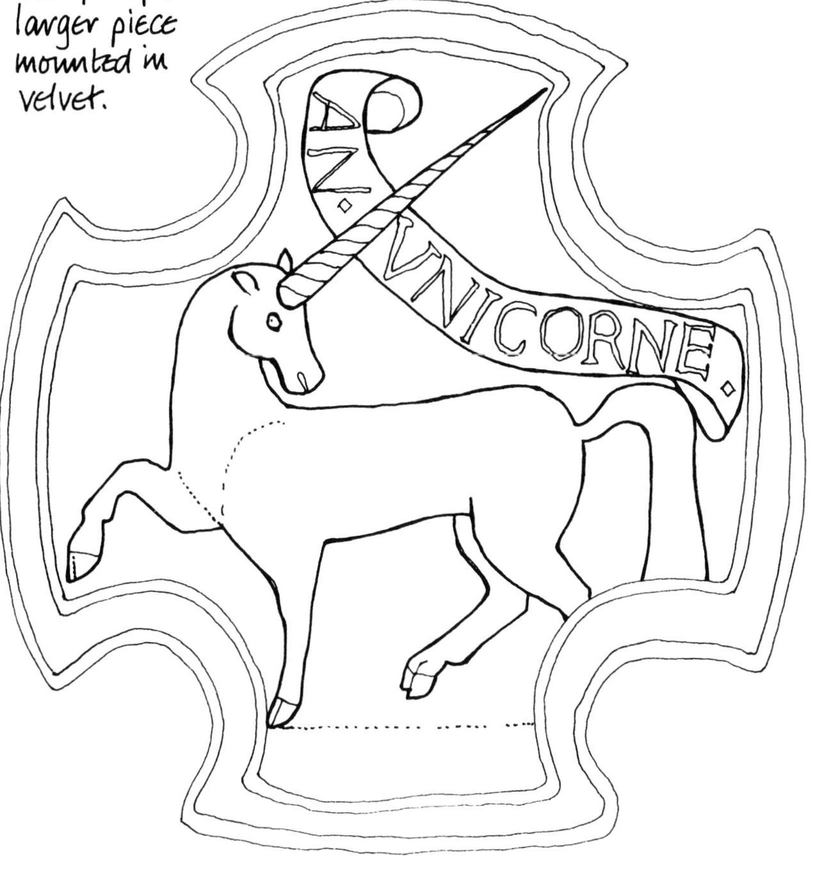


The Unicorn is one of many cruciform and octagonal panels embroidered in tent stitch by Mary, Queen of Scots while in captivity. With the lion, the design probably alludes to the royal arms of Scotland, though many of the others bear a more symbolic meaning which comment upon her future hopes.

Oxburgh Hall. Norfolk.

Detail of a scrolling pattern from a linen pillow-bere embroidered with coloured silks, silver-gilt and silver thread in chain, stem, plaited braid and buttonhole stitch, detached buttonhole-fillings and couching.

The flowers and fruit are those found in a sixteenth century garden, usually embroidered in their natural colours, carnation, rose, pansy, pomegranate, borage, pear, honeysuckle, campion and oak.

Unlike cushion-covers of the same period, pillow-covers are nearly always found without a border. They ceased to be made in the seventeenth century as the fashion had developed for embroidered drapes and curtains.

Victoria and Albert Museum.

The Bradford Table Carpet

Late 16th century

Large covers of canvas embroidery imitated the style of tapestries (hence the confusion of names) and covered plain wooden tables when these were not in use at meal times.

This well-known example in the Victoria and Albert Museum measures 13ft. × 5ft. 9ins. and is worked in fine tent stitch in silks on fine linen canvas. The centre is covered by a trellis of vines bearing grapes, and the wide border shows scenes of hunting, shooting, fishing and daily work, elegant buildings and the arts of gentle daliance by the nobility. Shown here are a water-mill, domestic buildings and a grand house with a moat and drawbridge, domes, and classical columns.

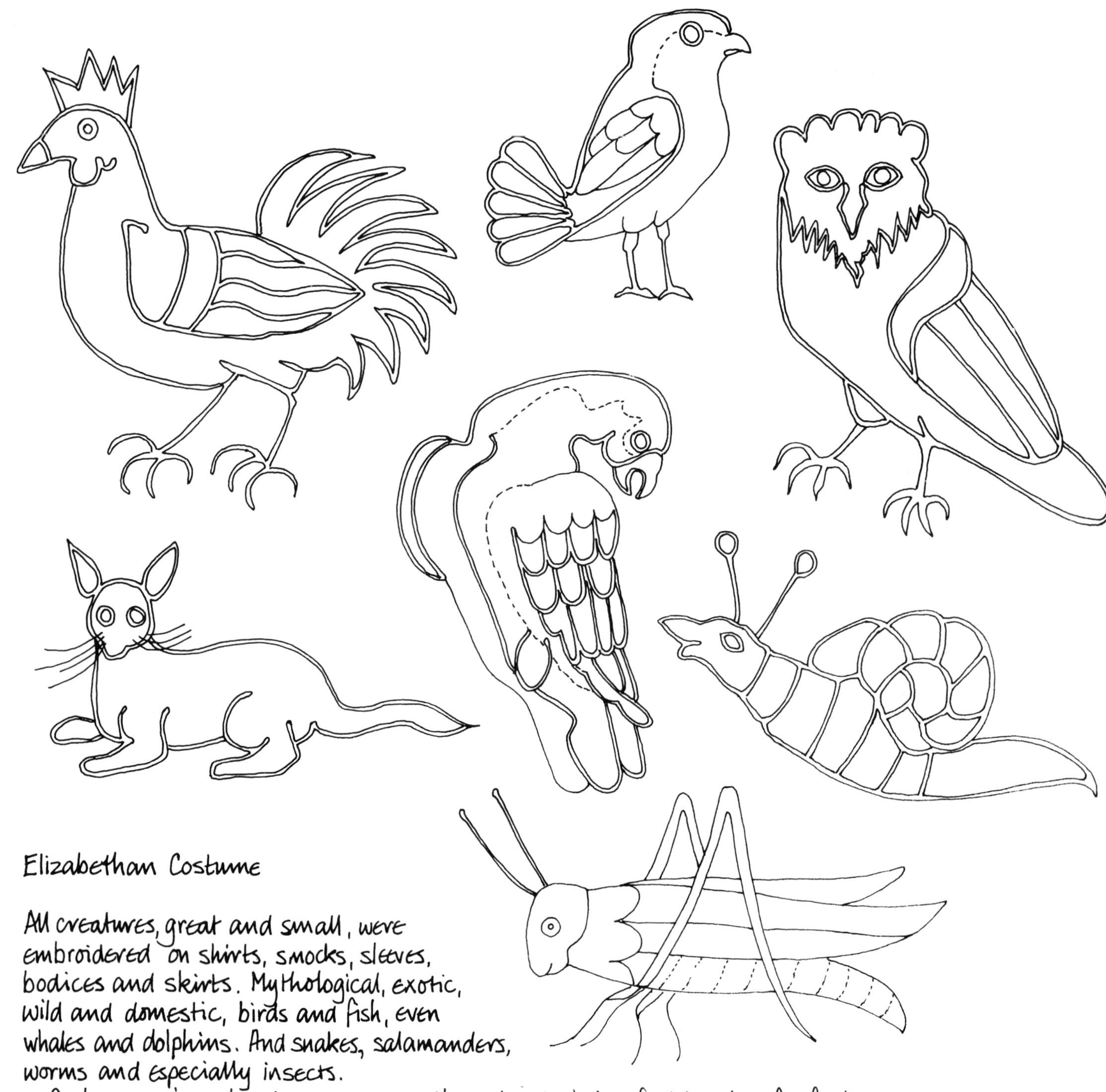

Elizabethan Costume

All creatures, great and small, were embroidered on shirts, smocks, sleeves, bodices and skirts. Mythological, exotic, wild and domestic, birds and fish, even whales and dolphins. And snakes, salamanders, worms and especially insects.

Scale was unimportant, more so was the value in being fashionable, for fashion spelled success.

The cockerel, sparrow, owl, cat, parrot and snail were embroidered in crimson silk on a white linen smock of c.1600. Victoria and Albert Museum. London.
The grasshopper was drawn out on a piece of linen, not worked. c.1600. Victoria and Albert Museum.

For the definitive book on the costumes of Queen Elizabeth I, see "Queen Elizabeth's Wardrobe Unlock'd." Janet Arnold. Published by Maney. ISBN 0 901286 20 6

This border is from a purse which once held the great seal of Elizabeth I. Embroidered in gold and silver threads on crimson velvet. British Museum.

"Teaching by sundry sortes of patterns and examples of different kindes, how to compose many faire works; which being set in order and forme according to the skill and understanding of the workman will, no doubt, yield profit unto such as live by the needle and give good content to adorne the worthy."

"Gentle Reader, I would have you know that the Diversitie of Examples which you shall find in this Schole House for the Needle are only but patterns which serve but to helpe and inlarge your invention. But for the disposing of them into form and order of workes that I leave to your own skill and understanding. Whose ingenious and well practised wits will soe readily (I doubt not) compose them into such beautiful formes as will be able to give content, both to the workers and the wearers of them."

"And again for your behoafs I have in the end of this booke made two scales or checker patterns which by enlarging or contracting into greater or lesser squares you may enlarge or make lesser any of the saide patternes and examples in the booke or any other whatever."

Excerpts from Richard Shorleyker's "A Schole House for the Needle" printed in Shoe Lane, London, "at the sign of the Faulcon." The first edition appeared in 1624. No perfect copy is known of this book, though three examples are known to exist, one in the Bodleian Library, Oxford, one in the Brussels Museum and one in the Victoria and Albert Museum, London.

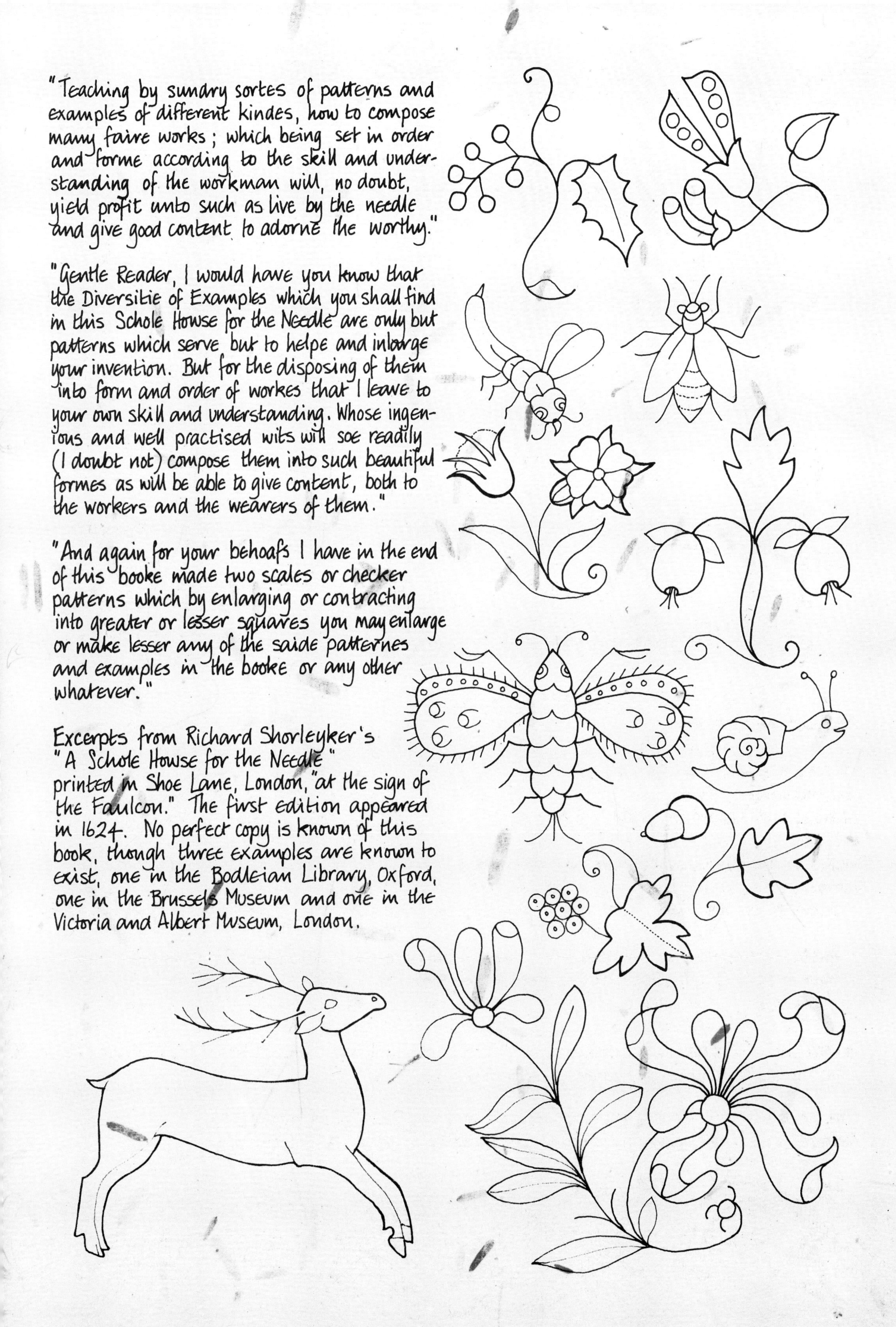

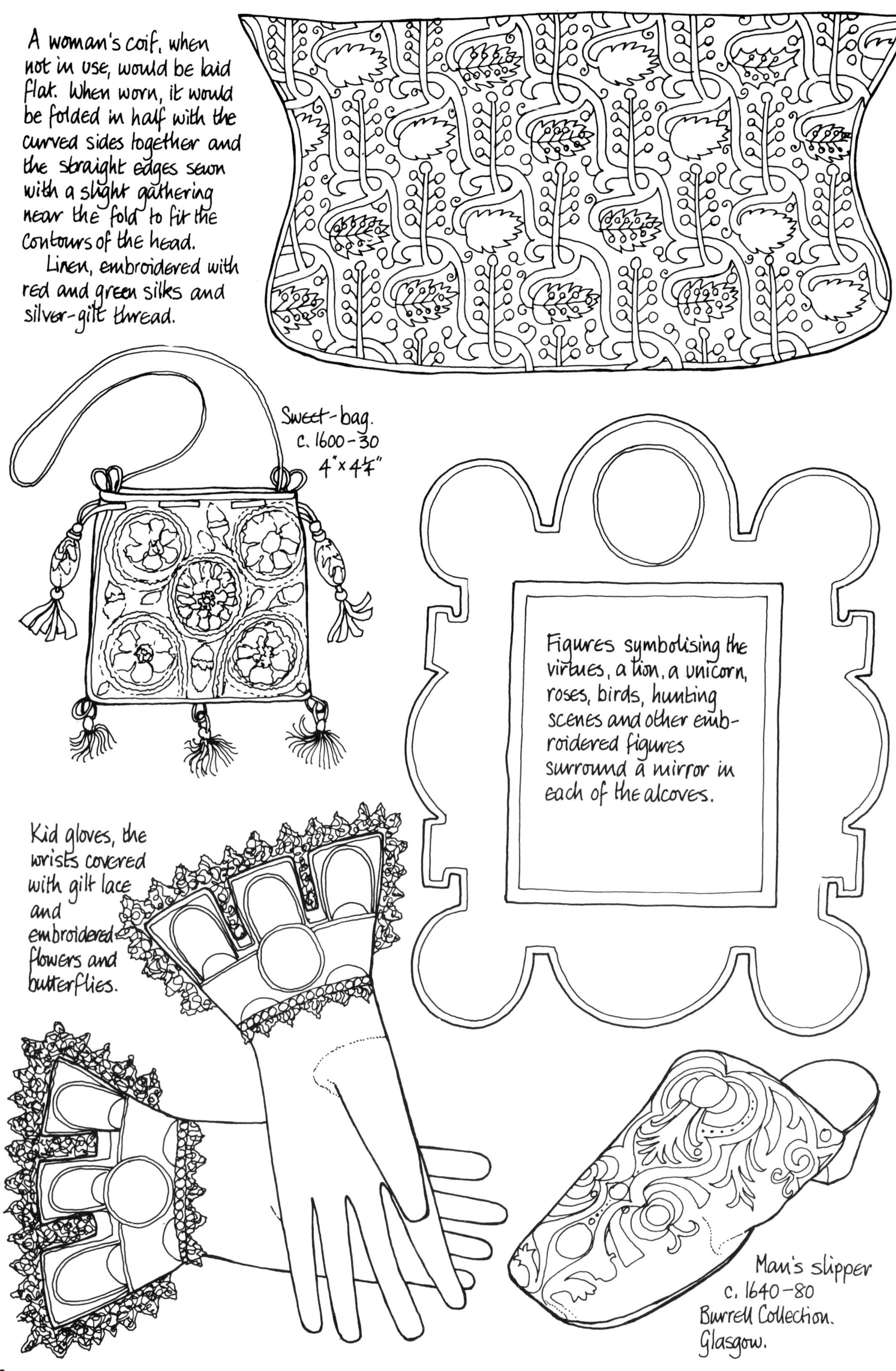
A woman's coif, when not in use, would be laid flat. When worn, it would be folded in half with the curved sides together and the straight edges sewn with a slight gathering near the fold to fit the contours of the head.
Linen, embroidered with red and green silks and silver-gilt thread.
Sweet-bag. c. 1600–30 4"×4¼"
Figures symbolising the virtues, a lion, a unicorn, roses, birds, hunting scenes and other embroidered figures surround a mirror in each of the alcoves.
Kid gloves, the wrists covered with gilt lace and embroidered flowers and butterflies.
Man's slipper c. 1640–80 Burrell Collection. Glasgow.

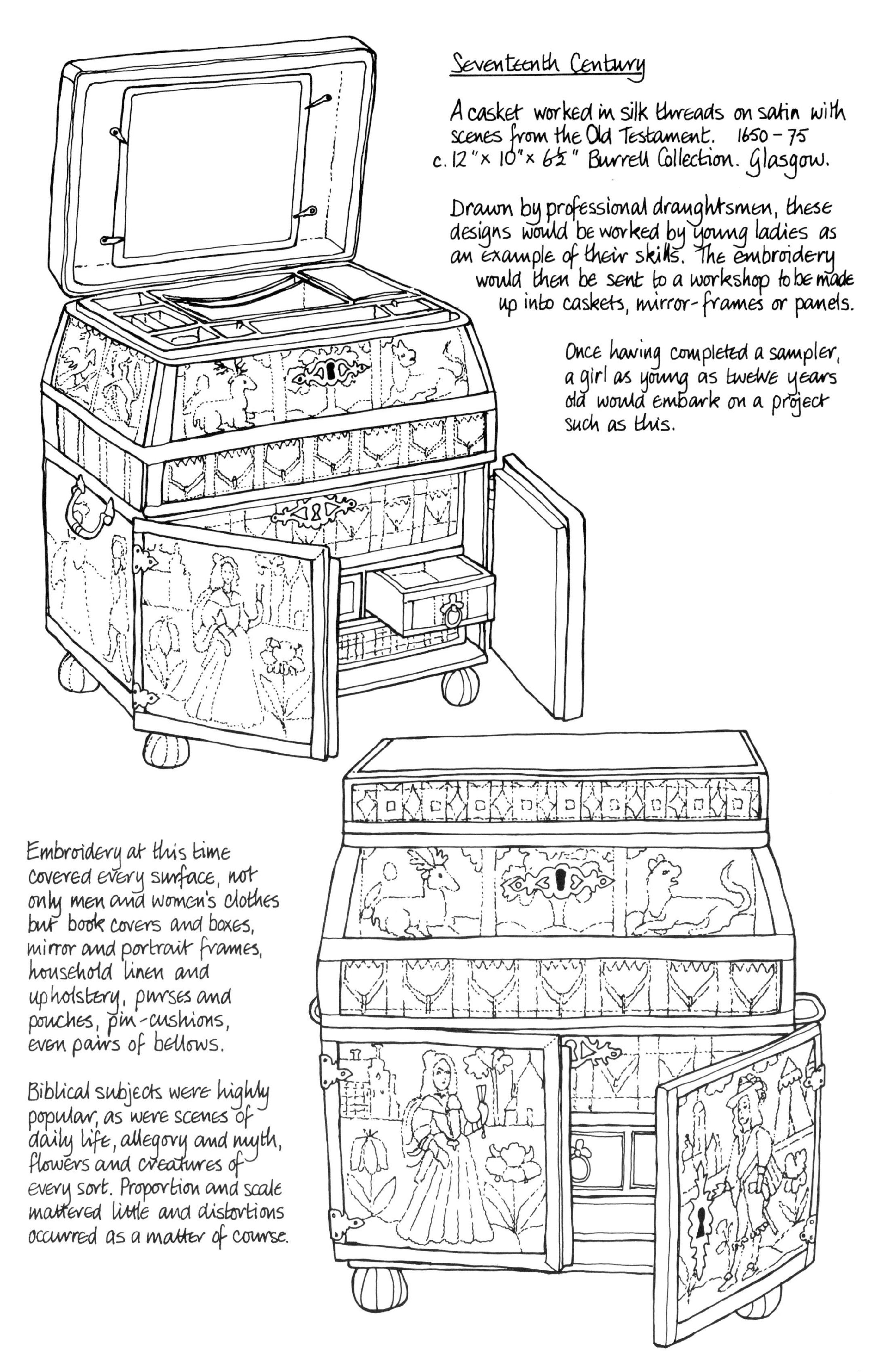

## Seventeenth Century

A casket worked in silk threads on satin with scenes from the Old Testament. 1650 – 75
c. 12" × 10" × 6½" Burrell Collection. Glasgow.

Drawn by professional draughtsmen, these designs would be worked by young ladies as an example of their skills. The embroidery would then be sent to a workshop to be made up into caskets, mirror-frames or panels.

Once having completed a sampler, a girl as young as twelve years old would embark on a project such as this.

Embroidery at this time covered every surface, not only men and women's clothes but book covers and boxes, mirror and portrait frames, household linen and upholstery, purses and pouches, pin-cushions, even pairs of bellows.

Biblical subjects were highly popular, as were scenes of daily life, allegory and myth, flowers and creatures of every sort. Proportion and scale mattered little and distortions occurred as a matter of course.

Knot patterns from 17th century English samplers as exercises in braiding

Below left: a design taken from a Swedish cushion cover of the 17th century. The eight-point star was one of the most popular motifs at this time.

"Pictures of men, birds, beasts and flowers,
When Leisure serv'd at idle hours,
All this rarely to the life,
As if there were a kind of strife
Twixt art and nature : trees of fruit
With leaves, boughs, branches, body, root
She made to grow in Winter time
Ripe to the eye.

Written of Susanna Perwich
c. 1643

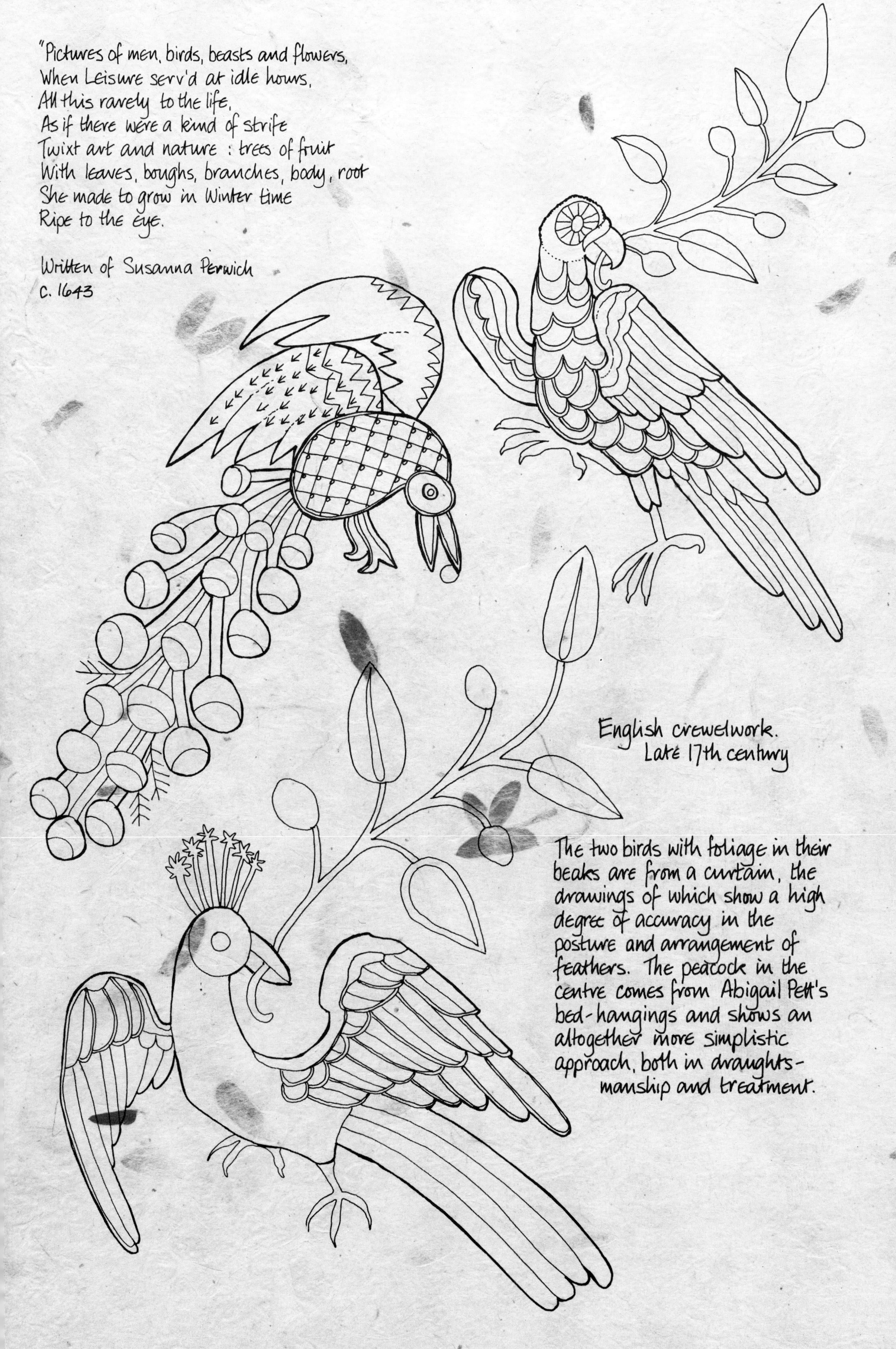

English crewelwork.
Late 17th century

The two birds with foliage in their beaks are from a curtain, the drawings of which show a high degree of accuracy in the posture and arrangement of feathers. The peacock in the centre comes from Abigail Pett's bed-hangings and shows an altogether more simplistic approach, both in draughtsmanship and treatment.

A pair of ribbed linen pockets embroidered in coloured wools and dated 1774. Manchester Art Gallery.

Below: cotton patchwork pocket with linen back. 15" x 12". American c.1780–1800

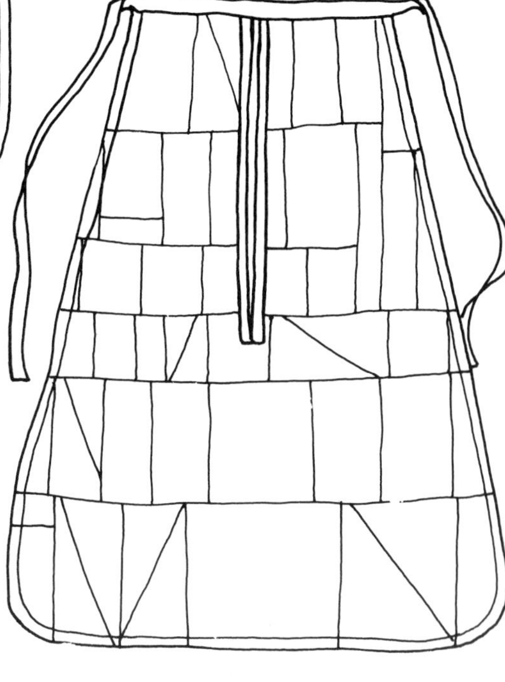

"Lucy Locket lost her pocket:
Kitty Fisher found it." Old English Rhyme.

"Stolen out of a Person's Pocket last Week, in the Common, a work'd Pocket-Book with a Pair of Stone Earrings, two Pair of Stone-Buttons which wanted mending, silver Thimble mark'd Hannah Bill, a large plain Stay-hook in the shape of a Heart, a silver Teaspoon broke off in the middle marked P.M. and sundry papers in it....."

Pockets, single or paired, were tied around the waist beneath the outer skirts, which had openings in the side-seams for access. Sometimes the tapes would come undone! The advertisement above illustrates what one such pocket contained, but among these items might have been a 'huswif' like a smaller version of the roll-up pouch, holding needles, thread and buttons.

The pocket-book might have been a single envelope with a squared or rounded flap, a double one that folded in the centre like the American canvaswork version shown on the left, or a roll-up like the multi-pouched one below. All these would have tied with lengths of tape attached at the flap or sometimes with a clasp of silver or other metal.

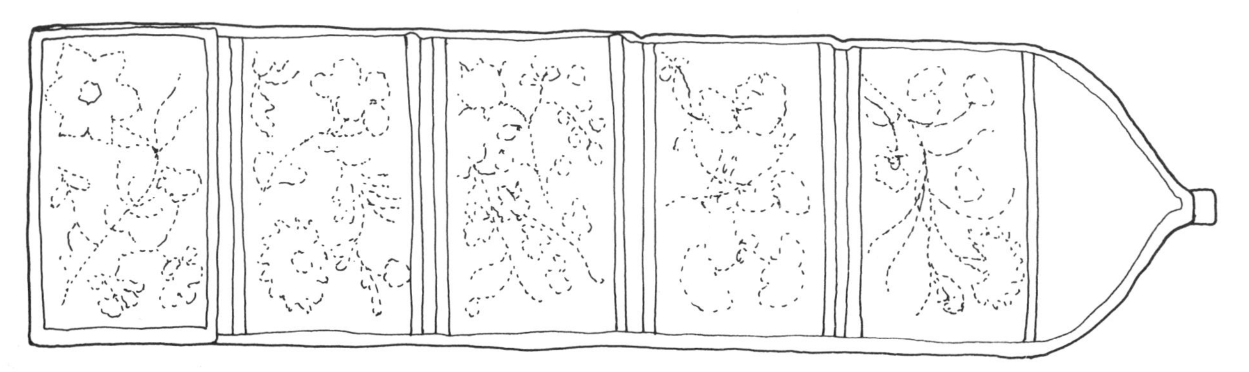

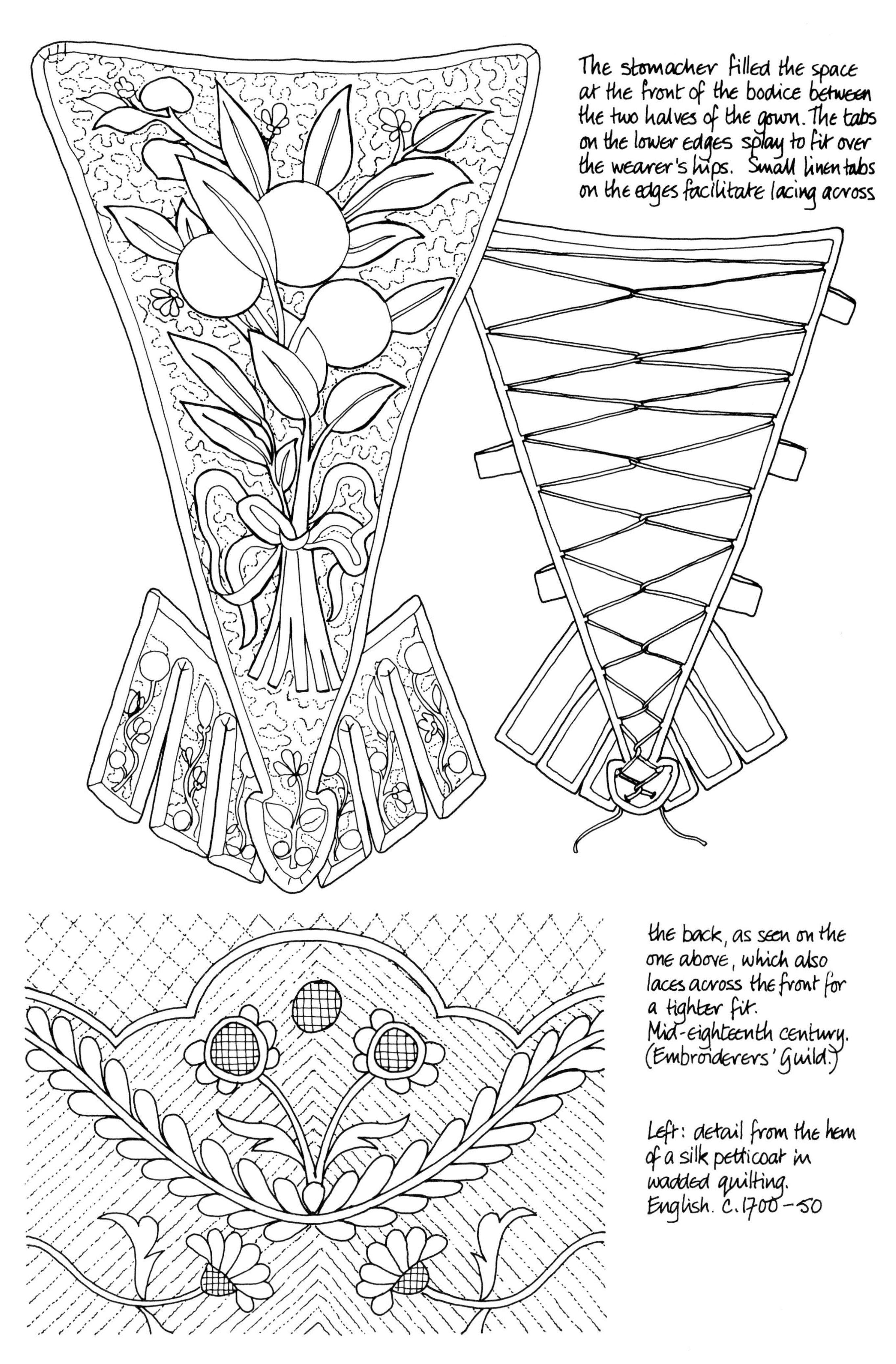

The stomacher filled the space at the front of the bodice between the two halves of the gown. The tabs on the lower edges splay to fit over the wearer's hips. Small linen tabs on the edges facilitate lacing across the back, as seen on the one above, which also laces across the front for a tighter fit. Mid-eighteenth century. (Embroiderers' Guild.)

Left: detail from the hem of a silk petticoat in wadded quilting. English. c.1700–50

Right: a bowl of fruit and their leaves from a French needlelace border of c. 1730.
Embroiderers' Guild Collection.

Below: a motif from a border of late eighteenth century Antwerp lace.

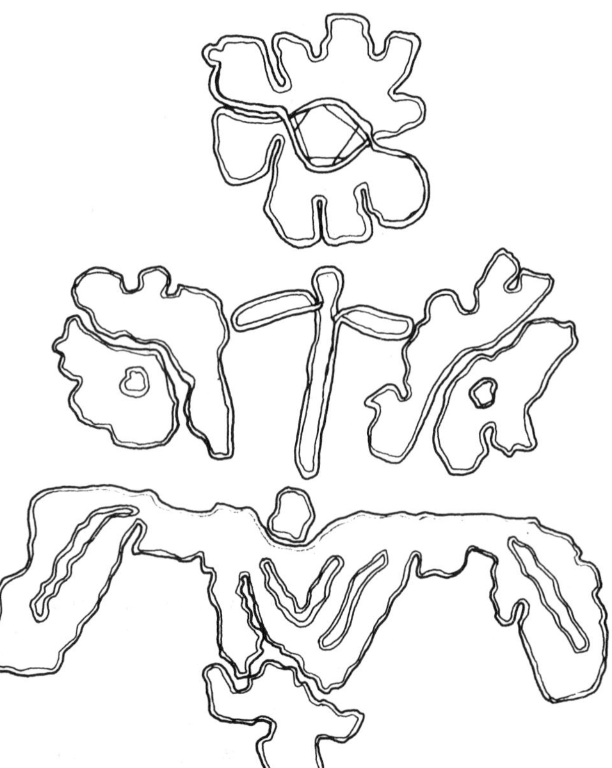

Advertisement in The Lady's Newspaper, May 31st. 1851

"Curlings, Court Lace Cleaners, 7 Duke Street, Grosvenor-square, beg to inform the Nobility and Gentry, that they Clean and Mend in the best possible manner every description of British and Foreign Lace. Brussels, Point, Honiton and other Flowers, elegantly arranged and appliquéd into Caps, Chemisettes, Collars, Berthes, Veils, Flounces, and &c. &c. on the newest shapes.
Court Plumes Cleaned and Mounted.
French Clear-starching in all its branches.
Silk dresses cleaned whole.
Pinking and Embossing done in the newest patterns."

Left: a simple motif from seventeenth century Flemish Mechlin lace of a potted plant on a ground known as fond d'armure because of its resemblance to chain mail.

Desirable Residence. Home of Miss Elizabeth Haines (initials over doorway) c.1720. A spacious accommodation with servants' quarters, extensive garden with flower beds in the latest style, urns on the patio, chequered forecourt and large wrought-iron gates. Upper balcony affords excellent view over surrounding parkland with oaks and wildlife. Tulips (the latest craze) a speciality at two hundred and fifty stitches to the inch. Classes given in silk on canvas, but bring own magnifying-glass for panels measuring no larger than 14 inches by 12½.
Promising students may exhibit in London sometime in the future. (V.+A. —author)

## Bibliography

The History of Textile Art. Agnes Geijer. pub. by Philip Wilson, London. 1979. and in U.S.A.
ISBN 0 85667 0553

Textiles in Archaeology. Wild. Shire Publications
Ancient Decorative Textiles. Violetta Thurstan (O.P.) The Favil Press.
Embroidery in Britain from 1200 – 1750. Victoria and Albert Museum Publications.
Embroidery: A History. Pamela Warner. Batsford.
English Domestic Needlework. Therle Hughes. Abbey Fine Arts (O.P.)
Furnishing Textiles. Pamela Clabburn. pub. by Viking for the National Trust.
Book of Needlework and Embroidery. pub. by Collins for the Royal School of Needlework
Embroidery 1600 – 1700 at the Burrell Collection (Glasgow) John Murray
The Needlework of Mary, Queen of Scots. Margaret Swain. Van Nostrand Rheinhold. (O.P.)

Others are mentioned in the text.

"Oct. 12th. 1784..... Married my old Maid Eliz. Claxton to Charles Cary..... She was dressed in a Linnen Gown that my niece gave her some time back."
From The Rev. James Woodforde's 'The Diary of a Country Parson.'

From 'The Draper and Haberdasher' J.W. Hayes 1878
p.29 "The haberdashery drawers should be frequently dusted out, kept well assorted, and the contents arranged in successive numbers from left to right or right to left, but avoid changing...... When colours are arranged in braids, reel cotton or sewing silks, never put purple by the side of blue, or blue by green, let some other colour intervene, the shades can then be more readily distinguished by gas light."

From a notice posted in Courtauld's Mills in 1860
"Licking Bobbins. When a Bobbin is fastened off, it has been a common practice to touch the end with the tongue to smooth it down, and there is no harm in that. But out of this practice has arisen another practice, both nasty and mischievous, of licking the Bobbins all over to make them weigh heavier. And to put an end at once, and altogether, to this nasty and mischievous practice of Licking the Bobbins, we now make it A RULE Not to touch the Bobbins with the Tongue at all; and the Overseers are hereby authorised to enforce this rule by Forfeits."

Opposite:
Two figures taken from the Devonshire Hunting Tapestries. 15th century. V.+A. London.